Everything Is BETTER
with a
GORILLA

ß

Everything Is BETTER
with a
GORILLA

Andrew Gall
Gorillastrations by Vince Soliven

Avon, Massachusetts

Published by Adams Media, a division of F+W Media, Inc.
57 Littlefield Street, Avon, MA 02322. U.S.A.
www.adamsmedia.com

ISBN 10: 1-4405-0390-7
ISBN 13: 978-1-4405-0390-0

Printed in China

10   9   8   7   6   5   4   3   2   1

Library of Congress Cataloging-in-Publication Data
is available from the publisher.

This publication is designed to provide accurate and
authoritative information with regard to the subject matter
covered. It is sold with the understanding that the publisher
is not engaged in rendering legal, accounting, or other professional advice. If legal advice or other expert assistance
is required, the services of a competent professional person
should be sought.

 —From a *Declaration of Principles* jointly adopted by a
Committee of the American Bar Association and
a Committee of Publishers and Associations

Many of the designations used by manufacturers and sell-
ers to distinguish their product are claimed as trademarks.
Where those designations appear in this book and Adams
Media was aware of a trademark claim, the designations
have been printed with initial capital letters.

*This book is available at quantity discounts for
bulk purchases.
For information, please call 1-800-289-0963.*

Andrew:

To Megan, whose proclamation that
"everything in the world would be better with gorillas"
was my inspiration for this book.

Vince:

To Shaleah, for always
supporting the right side of my brain.
And Sydney, for just being.

Everything Is Better with a Gorilla.

It's a simple statement, but it's indisputably true. Involving a Gorilla in pretty much every life situation will lead to good things. The pages of this book explore some of the millions of examples in which the inclusion of a Gorilla can turn the ordinary into the extraordinary.

Whether you're preparing to plan a wedding, organize an Olympic-caliber bobsled team, or anything in between, it's our hope that the lessons learned from this book will come in handy the next time you consider adding a Gorilla to the mix.

Don't say you've never thought about it.

Washing Dishes with a Gorilla

Washing dishes by yourself is no fun. Washing dishes with a Gorilla, however, is. Whenever the opportunity arises, you should wash dishes with a Gorilla.

Though Gorillas are large in stature, their demeanor is actually quite gentle, and despite their immensely powerful strength, they almost never break a dish. They also have a strong incentive to make your dishware spotlessly clean: Gorillas really enjoy looking at their reflections whenever possible.

Which Gorillas make the best dishwashing partners? Glad you asked.

Of all Gorilla species, Mountain Gorillas are the fuzziest. They grow especially thick coats due to the chilly high altitudes of their mountainous habitats. Their fuzziness enables you and your Gorilla to wash and dry sans dishtowels, as the Gorilla will just run the dishes across his massive body. You wash. The Gorilla dries. It's amazingly effective.

Wash dishes with a Gorilla by your side and you're doing the entire household a favor.

Inviting a Gorilla to Your House for a Sleepover

*d*espite your misgivings, you are never too old to have a sleepover. Especially when your guest weighs 400 pounds, walks on his knuckles, and is God's best creation of all time.

Gorillas are a ton of fun at sleepovers. They bring their favorite movies, their favorite blankets, and popcorn. Lots of popcorn. But the best thing (out of roughly 2,000 absolutely fantastic things) about having Gorillas sleep over is their self-sufficiency. In the wild, Gorillas build and sleep in "night nests"—a collection of leaves, branches, and thicket made into comfortable bedding, which they will sleep in for hours on end. Sleeping for hours on end is something Gorillas are extremely good at.

Letting a Gorilla spend the night is the perfect opportunity to have lots of one-on-one time—you can talk for hours and hours about your thoughts, fears, and wishes. Just know that at some point, the conversation will inevitably veer toward plants.

A Gorilla guest will treat your abode with the utmost respect and tender care, just like it's his very own night nest. Gorillas wash their own dishes, brew a morning pot of coffee, and will even grab the morning paper for you on their way out the next day.

Invite a Gorilla to sleep over. Your heart and soul won't soon regret it.

Taking a Walk with a Gorilla

gorillas love going on interesting walks. In fact, they spend the majority of their day strolling around in search of food. Think getting some fresh air is stimulating now? Just wait until you've got a 400-pound barrel of amazing by your side.

If you are concerned you won't be able to keep up with a Gorilla, you can take comfort in knowing that Gorilla walks tend to involve nearly as much resting as they do walking. Gorillas in the wild tend to rest in the mid-morning, afternoon, and mid-afternoon—pretty much guaranteeing that your walk with a Gorilla will be a leisurely one.

Gorillas are filled with an unrelenting love of nature, and walking with one will lead you to new sights, sounds, smells, and levels of extreme elation. Another thing you'll discover: a penchant for eating flowers.

After all the ambling, you might be tempted to knuckle walk in order to emulate your walking companion. However, few people can pull it off and it is not advisable unless you have a great deal of grace. Like Charlie Chaplin. He could probably do it.

Having a Gorilla as a Wingman

Whether it's a large group or a more intimate one, Gorillas pride themselves on togetherness. Their eating, sleeping, and traveling habits are all based upon what's best for their Gorilla group dynamic. In short, they look out for each other. For that reason, it should not surprise you to learn that Gorillas are the perfect wingmen.

Gorillas are polite, personable, and easygoing. They're very agreeable and are available to help you out whenever you need it—provided you buy the first round.

Gorilla wingmen (wing-Gorillas?) are a great way to attract attention, and also to break the ice. Think about it. "Hi, what's your name?" versus "Hey, look at how fuzzy my friend is—touch him!" Which works better?

It doesn't hurt that Gorillas have many fascinating stories to share, which will help keep the friend of your potential flame busy for as long as it takes you to make your move. Having a Gorilla as a wingman is akin to having a bowl of cereal in the morning. It just works.

*i*f you want to catch someone in a foot pursuit, you might think to call The Flash. While this is a good idea in theory, it is wrong—you should in fact call a Gorilla. (The Flash, of course, is actually a Gorilla in a man costume.)

Hot pursuits can mean many things. Fame. Riches. An additional piña colada. Whatever reason you choose to enter into them, they tend to be somewhat important. All the more reason to have a Gorilla pursuer at your disposal.

Gorillas have extensive pursuit experience from their upbringings. Gorillas young and old love playing a game called "chase," where they do just that for hours on end. They're used to lots of stopping, starting, and pursuing. Followed by extensive sleeping.

When it comes down to it, the best thing about having a Gorilla join you in the midst of a hot pursuit is the fact that you no longer actually have to do anything. Just ride like Gorilla infants do, dorsally (on the Gorilla's back) or ventrally (on the Gorilla's stomach), and let him catch up to the person whom you are chasing down.

Inevitably you will apprehend that person. What happens next is up to you. The Gorilla often prefers to make the fleeing party dance, but that's simply the Gorilla's preference (though you should probably honor it). Gorillas are non-violent, but will allow the use of chain mail armor in cases of extreme seriousness.

By the way, have you ever seen a Gorilla round a corner at full speed? It's absolutely poetic.

Seeking Counsel
from a Gorilla

You can talk to a Gorilla about virtually anything. Gorillas have an amazing capacity for empathy, and can always relate to your situation. For example, if you tell a Gorilla about being on a boat, the Gorilla will think about a time when he was on a boat, wearing one of those really comfortable sailing hats.

Gorillas are great advice givers, mainly because when it comes to living life, they've seen it all. Gorilla family and group dynamics can get quite complicated: Gorilla moms typically switch groups after her infants are old enough to be self-sufficient; juvenile Gorillas, meanwhile, switch groups when they reach Blackback age—usually, between the ages of eight and twelve—and start to lead groups of their own. This group swapping is a staple of Gorilla life. As a result, they are quite worldly.

They are also amazing listeners. Even when a Gorilla appears to be sleeping, he is still listening. (This also makes Gorillas the perfect audience for your vacation slides.) And Gorillas are very open-minded. They won't judge you or your problems as they listen, even if you're afraid to make eye contact. Or if you're obviously lying. Or if you're wearing penny loafers.

Sharing your innermost thoughts and fears with a Gorilla can be an extremely therapeutic experience.

Choosing a Gorilla as Your Running Buddy

*i*t's not easy to have the unwavering commitment required of dedicated fitness fanatics. When a Gorilla gets involved though, it's a whole new ballgame.

Whether quadrupedally (on all fours) or bipedally (upright, like people), Gorillas can cover a lot of ground in a hurry. And while they generally move at a leisurely pace, they can really get up and go when they need to, whether it's to solve conflicts, avoid danger, or get to some delicious plants in a timely manner. So if you're looking for some inspired running guidance, look no further.

Gorillas have been running distances short and long for many generations, and know exactly how much energy to use, as well as what programs yield the best results for weight loss, strength training, and giant calf progression.

Under the tutelage of Mr. Large, Hairy, and Amazing, not only will your running program be impactful, it will be interesting. Gorillas like to cover a diverse terrain when they run, so you're bound to discover lakes, trees, streams, rivers, and rockfaces you never knew existed. Then, they will stop and eat for eighteen hours, giving you ample time to rest and stretch.

Choose a Gorilla as your running buddy. The experience will make you equal parts physically fit and mentally astute.

Taking Acting Lessons
from a Gorilla

*i*f you wish to become a true method actor, the Gorilla school of acting is really where you should begin.

At a very young age, Gorillas learn by acting. They start emulating the actions of the older group members, honing skills they will eventually use as adults—actions like somersaulting, climbing, and swinging from vines. A Gorilla see, Gorilla do approach. They also learn how to communicate both verbally and nonverbally. Talk about thespians.

Gorillas are masters of the nuance. You will probably never know eyes can be so expressive until you look into theirs—you're likely to find all that you had previously been missing. At a Gorilla acting school you'll learn a variety of unique yet sensible techniques to master emoting through the eyes, one of which involves staring at a delicious houseplant for one-hour intervals.

Gorillas have seen overacting, and they hate it. If you make too much of a particular scene, you might be put on probation. Do it again, and you're that day's subject of derision, which mainly consists of being bluff-charged by the Gorilla staff all day long. Not fun, if you value clean underwear.

The Gorilla school of acting boasts many notable alumni, including Paul Newman, Robert Redford, and Johnny Depp, who does unpaid endorsements for the program, which you may have seen the last time you traveled to Sweden.

Sharing a Hug with a Gorilla

*g*orillas give the best hugs. Look at the size of their arms. The average wingspan of a Gorilla is nearly eight feet, which is much longer than the average human's. Some Gorillas could probably wrap their arms around you more than once. Imagine.

When you are hugging a Gorilla, it is wise to keep your mouth closed, as you don't want to swallow Gorilla fur while the two of you embrace. It would be an absolute tragedy to hug a Gorilla and choke on a Gorilla at the same time.

Hugging a Gorilla can make one feel superhuman. After hugging a Gorilla, feel free to go dunk that basketball. Or reason with that boss. Or lift that car above your head.

Envelop yourself in the gentle, warming embrace of a Gorilla and let your cares and worries disappear.

Hiring a Gorilla to Help Rid You of Your Ant Infestation Problem

*P*reviously, you might not have considered enlisting a Gorilla to help you rid your home of ants. That, of course, was then.

Gorillas make great exterminators. This is a proven fact, given that in the wild, Gorillas are known for eating ants as a source of protein. They're insatiable, in fact. Often, the entire Gorilla family joins in, scooping up ants by the handful and consuming them joyously. Great fun.

Thanks to their experience in the wild, Gorillas know all the tricks of the extermination trade, from flushing out the ants to coaxing them out of hiding via gentle wood whittling.

One advantage is that Gorillas don't need tools to eradicate the ants from your house. This will save you thousands of dollars in potential extermination costs. Though you should know, Gorillas have been known to charge for their services, then spend it all on manicures. (It's all a part of being presentable.) Fewer tools also means less of a contamination risk for both you and the Gorilla.

Chances are, once you've teamed up with a Gorilla to eliminate the ant infestation in your home, you're going to want to do it again in others' homes. This could lead to the possible formation of a partnership where the Gorilla eliminates ants for customers and you run the business affairs. Just think of the advertising possibilities—low-budget cable commercials where you and the Gorilla dress as Dutchmen, for example.

If nothing else, the memory of accomplishing something with the help of the most amazingly massive yet symmetrically faced mammal one has ever had the pleasure of knowing will put a smile on your face in the morning.

Working with a Gorilla to Help Train Your Child Prodigy

*d*o you feel like your child is especially talented far beyond his or her years? Then this is your chance to foster those gifts.

In the wild, young Gorillas thrive by emulation, picking up adult traits at an amazingly young age. Lucky them. And lucky you, if you can get your child prodigy in to see a Gorilla while he or she is still young and impressionable.

Taking your child prodigy to a Gorilla early-education specialist can lead to astounding things. Mozart, Dostoyevsky, and the majority of Austin, Texas all went to see Gorillas at a young age, mainly at the urging of their parents (except in the case of Mozart, who went completely on his own).

Gorilla prodigy overseers will take your child through a variety of cognitive drills, including naming state capitals and the first forty-six numerals of pi. Though it all begins with introductory French lessons, of course.

If you're lucky, your child will take to the Gorilla adviser immediately, and if nothing else, pick up the habits of a typical Gorilla, including long periods of sleeping, eating healthy vegetarian meals, and the general ability to be remarkable.

Do your child a favor and get him or her involved with a Gorilla as soon as humanly possible. If you can pull it off, you really should have a Gorilla present at the birth.

*i*t's not often that mere men receive the privilege of meeting an esteemed leader of a nation. All the more reason that when this honor is bestowed on you, it's best to have a Gorilla in tow.

Gorillas in general, and in particular Silverbacks—mature adult males—are often described as regal themselves. This is mostly due to their disposition and propensity to strut. Indeed, it is quite an impressive sight. In fact, this may be the only occurrence where the king, queen, tsar, duke, or prince you've come to visit may actually bow to you instead.

Gorillas know how to act around the upper crust of society. Some examples of blue-blooded behavior that you might not be aware of—but that Gorillas are well versed in—include opening pistachios with their stomachs, drinking water through clenched teeth, and putting mustard on everything.

Having a Gorilla go with you will enable you to get closer to said royalty than ever before. The handlers, special service workers, and other assorted royal underlings trust a Gorilla like they trust their own mothers, allowing you to therefore get much, much closer.

Gorillas have a history with roughly all the current leaders of the free world, and often serve as go-betweens when mediating conflicts or diffusing potential international incidents. For that reason, expect a fruit basket filled with dozens of bananas as a thank-you present for bringing such an enlightened and esteemed guest. Enjoy.

Visiting
Royalty with
a Gorilla

Going to the Movies
with a Gorilla

*g*oing to the movie theater with a Gorilla can be quite an enjoyable experience. Gorillas possess a keen ability to just lay around, take it easy, and eat—so you can rest assured that two hours with one in a darkened theater isn't exactly going to cause a ruckus. Also, you won't have to worry about them talking during the movie—another plus.

It's a well-known fact that Gorillas are true cinephiles, and possess excellent judgment as film critics. Every Gorilla has seen *Citizen Kane* at least 100 times, and *Ishtar* less than three.

Gorillas, like other avid movie critics, can get quite animated when discussing their favorite films. If you really want to get a Gorilla riled up, talk about how transcendent Jar Jar Binks is. You'll be treated to a full-on chest beating display.

While Gorillas prefer movies on the big screen, they do enjoy the occasional DVD, and still make good use of video. Also, they really thought Laserdisc was going to take off. Don't hold that against them the next time you watch a film.

Square Dancing with a Gorilla

Country western line dancing may have peaked a few decades back, but square dancing is alive and well, thanks to a recent explosion in Gorilla participants. The experience of square dancing with a Gorilla is an art form that, if not of utmost world importance, is certainly on par with the need to be diplomatic with Russia.

Gorillas are quite coordinated on the dance floor. This stems from the fact that in the wild Gorillas are known for making very calculated movements, whether it's a display, bluff, or full-blown charge. These movements define the Gorilla's physical being in everyday life. Not surprisingly, this translates to an amazingly fluid whirlwind of allemandes, two-steps, and do-si-dos.

A Gorilla's fancy footwork is equaled only by his gentle demeanor and Boy-Scout-like level of attention offered to his square dance partner. Getting spun by a Gorilla is best described as plunging through a portal of silky chocolate and landing on a soft feather crash pad that smells of lilacs.

Underrated: The way Gorillas look in oversized belt buckles.

If this factual analysis doesn't convince you to jump up and square dance with a Gorilla at precisely this moment, a variety of instructional videos featuring Gorillas square dancing are available online as visual persuasion. Better start Googling.

Building the World's Largest Human/Gorilla Pyramid

*m*any people aspire to achieve world records that will live on in the annals of history. A slightly smaller group of these individuals aspire to achieve world records involving Gorillas. A few words of advice: Join this smaller group.

Building a world-record-setting human/Gorilla pyramid is no easy task. Lucky for you, Gorillas are great climbers, making it easy to grow your pyramid to its highest, most record-breaking heights. Being stood on by a Gorilla is one of the highest honors a mortal can receive, just ahead of being knighted.

Because Gorillas are efficient, you'll get your pyramid built in a timely manner, enabling you to spend the rest of the day comparing your experience with other high points of your life. Like when world peace was achieved, or the time you met Mario Andretti.

Gorillas know the *Guinness Book of World Records* people very well. And since Gorillas are quite dependable when it comes to setting world records, no *Guinness* representative will rush you or maintain anything less than a professional demeanor during your record attempt—they know that when a Gorilla is involved, it's time to get serious.

Your participation in the world's largest human/Gorilla pyramid is sure to bring you fame, fortune, and assorted rare jewels. Be generous with your wealth, won't you?

Getting a Gorilla to Mediate Your Disputes with Others

Conflict resolution with a Gorilla tends to be a very engaging experience. It's a matter of who's right, who's wrong, and who eats more tree bark.

Silverbacks have a great deal of experience in the world of conflict mediation. As the leaders of large groups of Gorillas, Silverbacks must keep order among the members, resolving disagreements on issues ranging from food to mating to whose chest beats sound better. Suddenly, that little argument about who left the toilet seat up seems amazingly trivial.

When you ask a Gorilla to mediate, expect a swift and just hearing—one in which both sides will be listened to fairly.

If you talk out of turn, watch out. Gorillas aren't afraid to put you in your place if you become unruly. Making you wear funny hats, like the kind you see on pirates, is certainly within the realm of punishment for such disruptions.

It's a little-known fact that due to their experience as conflict mediators, Gorillas currently run twenty-seven countries within the U.N.—including many of the world's powerhouses. Those twenty-seven are among the world's leaders in GDP, import-to-export ratio, and total bananas harvested.

In the end, a dispute mediated by a Gorilla is sure to result in a solution that is of utmost satisfaction to both parties—not to mention society as a whole. With that, let's all join hands.

Hiring a Gorilla as Your Financial Adviser

*i*f you're looking for smart financial planning with a touch of levity, look no further than a Gorilla. Gorillas have the skill set and financial market understanding you need to keep yourself in good financial shape well into your retirement years.

The key to financial wisdom lies in an understanding of efficiency. Do Gorillas possess such an understanding? You bet. When Gorillas forage for food, they find a place they like, consume anything and everything they can, then return a few weeks or months later. And by the time they do, the vegetation they pillaged has grown back more plentiful and delectable than ever before. Voilà—delicious, delicious efficiency.

When it comes to money, the outlook of a Gorilla is pretty simple: Don't spend what you don't have. It's a mantra they themselves practice, and a group of Gorillas even wrote a self-help book by the same name. (Though it was a book dedicated to painting rather than finance.)

Take your financial questions to a Gorilla and he will get you set up with the right stocks and bonds to maximize your income while minimizing your penalties. Gorillas feel really good about Roth IRAs, less so about T-bills. Due to their foresight, no Gorillas were sucked into the subprime mortgage fiasco of 2007–08.

Inviting a Gorilla to Be a Guest on Your Talk Show

*i*f you have a talk show, you understand the importance of charisma in regards to entertainment value. And if you understand the importance of charisma in regards to entertainment value, you know that having a Gorilla on your talk show would be the absolute tops.

Gorillas have charisma in spades, Silverbacks in particular. It is, in fact, the key to their leadership ability. It's how they attract, and continue to attract, females and additional group members. The female Gorillas want them. The male Gorillas want to be them. People listen to (and, in fact, want to be) Gorillas as well. That is, of course, because all of their opinions and worldviews are indisputably correct. Whether they're discussing hunger in third-world countries or violence in inner cities, Gorillas are astonishingly articulate, with mountains of well-thought-out ideas that would make an ordinary man tremble with amazement.

It doesn't hurt that they also have the physical presence of six times your average emperor. This is an especially important distinction when it comes time to prepare your talk show set for a Gorilla appearance—they're so passionate about which they speak, they're as likely to make a pronouncement while climbing your ceiling as they are while sitting in your comfy chair.

Unlike Howard Beale in *Network*, Gorillas will not use being on television as a medium to be exploited for their personal gain. And unlike Andy Rooney, Gorillas will never sound like a crotchety old man—nor will they have unwieldy eyebrows.

TV viewers from Portsmouth to Portugal would be wise to tune into any televised discourse with nature's hairy miracle, and as talk show host, you should allow your viewers this pleasure frequently—after all, even you could learn a thing or two.

Juggling with a Gorilla

gorillas are excellent jugglers. This fact, of course, goes without saying.

How do Gorillas juggle so well? Aside from a strong showing in the field of general awesomeness, Gorillas have the dexterity and hand-eye coordination necessary to keep multiple objects in the air at the same time, be it bowling pins, chainsaws, or lawn chairs.

As a Gorilla's juggling partner, study his eyes to find out when to move to the next trick. Gorillas possess a wide variety of nonverbal communication skills, from head and mouth movements to hand gestures. Considering how interesting their family dynamics can be, it's no wonder that they possess such a wide range of signals to help them interact as both individuals and groups. (Essentially, it's like a really hairy episode of *The Waltons*.) At any rate, their innate skills allow Gorillas and their juggling partners to move effortlessly from trick to trick. Try to keep up.

Even if an onlooker tries to distract a Gorilla while objects are flying, the Gorilla will not succumb to those sideshow diversions. Gorillas are used to concentrating supremely at all times.

Perfect a juggling act with a Gorilla and you'll be the center of attention at any festival, party, or sidewalk. Get *really* good and the Gorilla can start juggling you. That's pretty fun.

Listening to Records with a Gorilla

*i*t is not surprising that Gorillas are more sonically proficient than us humans. In daily life, it is difficult for Gorillas to see long distances, as their line of vision is often blocked by dense vegetation. As a result, hearing plays an important role in Gorillas locating each other, detecting danger, and generally thriving in their environments. Further, Gorillas communicate using a number of vocalizations, nuanced in ways that only Gorillas and their superior listening skills would be able to understand.

They are also huge music trivia buffs. Go ahead, test a Gorilla's knowledge of any particular genre. From R&B to rock 'n roll to rockabilly to washboarding, Gorillas know every significant event that has occurred in music since the beginning of time.

Gorillas, like DJs, are often known as "crate diggers," spending hours in a record store's dusty basement in order to uncover rare treats, b-sides, and unreleased recordings. Interestingly, Gorillas are also known to collect cassette singles, and were very sad when the Warehouse of Music stopped stocking them.

When it's time to check out a Gorilla's record collection, your only limitation is time. That, and your appetite for esteemed knowledge.

Running a Daycare with a Gorilla

*t*aking care of multiple children simultaneously can be a daunting task. Hiring a Gorilla to help run your daycare is a chance to watch and learn from a master.

Gorilla mothers are amazingly adept at rearing infants. They help their infants learn to eat the right foods and build the right nests to sleep in, while letting the babies ride around on their backs to help them find their way in the world. And unless you have grown to be 400 pounds of magnificence, the results of their rearing are indisputably superior to yours.

From the moment she clocks in, your Gorilla daycare partner will get to work, folding towels, changing diapers, and spinning mobiles—all at the same time. The dexterity of both a Gorilla's fingers and toes allow for more efficient movement and action. And nothing is better music to infant ears than a lullaby delivered entirely in Gorilla grunts.

Gorillas are also great at dealing with parents. Their soothing voice and easy demeanor give potential clients a sense of trust. If you're already running a daycare with a Gorilla, you might also want to consider starting a Gorilla au pair service, as parents will undoubtedly want a Gorilla in their homes around the clock. It's a no-brainer.

Going Sailing with a Gorilla

When you're on a boat with a Gorilla, you'll need more than a life vest to prepare yourself. You'll also need a fifty-gallon drum of awe, amazement, and fascination. In equal parts, of course.

You might be interested to know that while Gorillas don't generally drink water (they get all they need from the vegetation they eat), they certainly have an affinity for it, as Mountain and Lowland Gorillas have been observed standing, sitting, and splashing in lakes and ponds from time to time. No word on whether or not they play Marco Polo.

A favorable attitude toward water combined with a general sense of awesomeness makes any Gorilla a master of the high seas. They can instinctively tell which direction they are facing, and are, in essence, walking compasses.

Not only can Gorillas navigate, they have also memorized the coordinates of every island in the world, from Guam to South Sandwich, and can give you a guided tour of any bit of landscape you happen to come across—no map needed. What's more is that Gorillas are masters of diplomacy, which will come in handy should you find yourself dealing with other boats, the Coast Guard, or lonely pirates.

Go sailing with a Gorilla. It really is a day at the beach.

Playing Poker
with a Gorilla

*h*airy bodies. Big bellies. Soft, understanding eyes. What could Gorillas possibly know about gambling? Anything and everything, for starters.

Like covering peanuts with chocolate, sitting at a poker table with a Gorilla by your side is a recipe for success. First off, Gorillas are masters in the art of bluffing. Most Gorillas (especially Silverbacks) use this bluffing skill in the wild when charging a potential enemy. Though a Gorilla barreling toward you at a high speed is generally cause for concern (and how), most Gorilla charges are actually bluffs to scare, intimidate, and generally get the bluffee moving in the opposite direction. And Great Caesar's Ghost, is it successful.

When gambling, Gorillas don't tend to bet large sums of money—they simply buy in and end up winning out, every time. Their bluffing skills cancel out any need for a poker face. Not that it matters—there's too much fur on their faces to make heads or tails of what they're thinking anyhow.

Gorillas are quite observant at the card table, and can read a tell like an open book. No twitch, blink, or hand gesture is safe. They've seen it all before, and if it happens, they'll call a fellow player on it.

When it's time to collect your winnings, no pit boss would ever consider hassling you and your Gorilla poker partner, as one wrong move could wind up turning the name on the door of the establishment from Carl's Cards, Coins, and Chips to The Silverback Sojourn.

Enlisting a Gorilla as your poker playing partner—it's a matter of simple common sense.

Conducting a Surveillance Operation with a Gorilla

*i*t's hard to imagine that something so large, so fuzzy, and so blatantly awesome could ever go undetected, but it's true.

Assuming your surveillance operation requires more than a day's worth of tracking, Silverback surveillance is probably the way to go. Lone Silverbacks will track other Gorilla groups in the wild. This helps them gain intel on the other Gorillas and plan out how to take some of the group's females and build their own groups.

Like building a Rube Goldberg machine, surveillance is long and complicated, requiring a workman-like commitment to excellence and a surgeon-like (rather than sturgeon-like)

attention to detail. Of course, a Gorilla possesses both of these highly valued characteristics.

If a Gorilla suspects his surveillance operation has been compromised, it's no problem. Gorillas can dispose of their documentation and evidence in seconds in the nearest dense vegetation. Sometimes, however, Gorilla detectives, in a hungry state, decide to ravage the very same vegetation in which the evidence lies. At this point, all bets are off.

Gorillas, like all great P.I.s, like to build a cache of evidence before making their move. Expect photos, charts, and a load of audio and video. Best of all, Gorilla P.I. evidence is always admissible in court. Your case is airtight, counselor.

Playing Catch with a Gorilla

*a*s you probably know, Gorillas tend to walk on their knuckles. While knuckle-walking is undeniably a great way to get around, there are other benefits too: namely, strong hands. And with those strong hands comes the ability to perfect and master a number of baseball grips—grips that the average man alone would struggle to master.

On the baseball field, the Gorilla's rare combination of power and speed has not been seen since the likes of the Cincinnati Reds' "Big Red Machine" teams of the 1970s. Pitching-wise, Gorillas are basically a hybrid of all 300 game winners in the history of the sport, only fuzzier.

Playing catch with a Gorilla can be a real learning experience.
You'll be taught a variety of pitches, from sliders and curves
to shutos, eephuses, and the infamous celeryball—a pitch that
seems to dart from left to right then back again.

Though you will never be able to pitch
as well as a Gorilla, your baseball
throwing will inevitably be improved
following a game of catch with one.
It's like throwing the ball around with
your dad. If your dad was Zeus.

Inviting a Gorilla to Help You Learn the Family Business

the family business can be difficult, but also extremely rewarding. Learning the trade of one's father (and often, one's grandfather) can put you in the position to succeed. Of course, this all comes together best under the tutelage of a Gorilla's watchful eye.

Gorillas observe and report like no other mammals, telling you which practices of your family's business you should continue, and which ones you should discard. For example, the tradition of handing out lollipops to customers. According to a Gorilla, you should definitely continue this one.

If you're worried a Gorilla could get between you and the legacy you've built with your family members, don't. Gorillas know how to talk to the old grizzled vets of industries the world over, and are experts on the latest and greatest business philosophies and technological innovations.

Provided the companies aren't run on an accrual accounting method.

What's more, a Gorilla knows exactly when it's the right time to retire. Many Silverbacks lead their groups until they are replaced by a successor, who is often their son. Yet again, this emulation of Gorilla behavior is certainly recommended. And they can help to convince your father that it's time to step aside and hand you the reins. Gorillas usually find it best to communicate this through a series of charts.

When you enlist a Gorilla to help you learn the family business, it's sort of like hiring a consultant, only the consultant makes the job look so magnificent you may decide you want to be a consultant rather than learn the family business. Gorillas are surprisingly fine with this, provided you're reaching your full economic potential.

Playing on a Seesaw with a Gorilla

gorillas are the ultimate partners in all playground activities. They enjoy slides, swings, and eating wood chips. Though they don't much care for monkey bars.

The penultimate Gorilla playground activity? Teeter-tottering. Gorillas make fantastic teeter-totter companions. This is a function of their surprising agility, given their size. Gorillas can climb trees, swing on vines, walk and run bipedally, do somersaults, play leapfrog, master air guitar, plié, and simultaneously pat their heads while rubbing their stomachs. Nothing, however, quite compares to being across from one on a seesaw. Forget fast and large motorcycles: When you playground seesaw with a Gorilla, you are truly in for the ride of your life.

As you take a seat on the teeter-totter across from the Supreme Being of the Playground, take a moment to observe the power of the universe at work—*you are about to teeter-totter with a Gorilla*. Movies have been made about far less.

Gorillas are also masters of nonverbal communication. So when you want to go up, just give a look. When you want to go down, give another look. It's that simple.

Occasionally, Gorillas lose interest in teeter-tottering. This generally happens when foliage is nearby. Regardless, they will still humor you. They're really good at humoring you. They're such givers.

*g*orillas pride themselves on being "fun maximizers," ensuring that you spend less time planning and more time actually doing. Do you imagine that Gorillas are also quite excellent at making difficult decisions, like choosing between French fries, salad, or baked potato as a dinner side? Because that is precisely what you should imagine. (The correct choice is salad, of course.)

Gorillas make decisions quickly and emphatically. After a group of Gorillas have been eating for a while, the leader will grunt to see if the majority of the group is done feeding. If most grunt back, the group ends their feeding and moves on. True democracy at work.

Gorillas are masters of making you decisive about your indecisions. They offer around a dozen simple ways to make a choice, all of which are more universally fair than flipping a coin, which is biased against the wrist-deprived.

Gorillas hate to become exasperated with your lack of decision-making ability, but sometimes it is simply inevitable. In this case, the Gorilla pulls out a didgeridoo and encourages you to join in a freestyle jig—this is a sight worth seeing, even if you are actually an excellent decision maker.

A Gorilla once advised a head of state on a potentially difficult decision concerning international diplomacy. Peace broke out, and the clouds rained star fruit.

Asking a Gorilla to Recommend the Latest Hip Restaurant

*i*t goes without saying that Gorillas are giant foodies. From leaves to nettles to wild celery, Gorillas are constantly on the lookout for the choicest foodstuffs. Once they discover where the best food is, they wind up returning—not just often, but very often.

Did you know that Gorilla restaurant-finding information tends to come mainly from new media? I'm sorry if you did not. Gorillas are constantly checking blogs, Facebook groups, e-mail notifications, MySpace postings, and Tweets for information on the latest restaurants in their local area, which is usually either near a rainforest or a roundabout.

Gorillas like to check out restaurants for themselves before reporting back to their friends. Usually a Gorilla enjoys impeccable service, due largely in part to the fact that he is a Gorilla. Gorillas have the ability to see through false pretenses, however, and if it all seems like a sham the Gorilla will get up and leave without paying.

Gorillas have also appeared as guest judges on every season of the Bravo reality series *Top Chef*. Unsurprisingly, these Gorilla guest appearances have also been the highest Nielsen-rated shows of each respective season.

The next time you're looking for a new restaurant to visit, (knuckle) walk over to a Gorilla and find out. You'll get a fair, unbiased review that's sure to satisfy.

The meatballs depicted here are, of course, made of tofu. As Gorillas are vegetarians, this goes without saying. But you already knew that, because you've been paying attention. Carry on, good reader.

Traveling Europe with a Gorilla

*h*eading to far-away lands like Lisbon, Slovenia, and Prague with a Gorilla can be a life-changing experience. So much culture to see. So much history to digest. So much vegetation to consume.

Travel companions can be a crapshoot. But when you travel with a Gorilla, you know what you're getting into—something awesome. Gorillas always travel light, as they tend to utilize the land's resources for all their needs, including food and shelter. Which means goodbye heavy backpack, hello nature's greatest beast.

Another plus: Gorillas pride themselves on being up for anything. Theater. Dancing. Museums. Even the odd street performance group. Regardless of what part of the European culture you choose to immerse yourself in, your Gorilla travel companion will be by your side.

One thing to look out for when traveling Europe with a Gorilla: You will get a lot of attention. Reverence for Gorillas is not limited to stateside, and it is common for Europeans to approach with great fanfare, in a haphazard manner, and demand pictures, autographs, autographed pictures, grooming tips, cups of coffee, and massages from any Gorilla they see on their cobblestone streets. Luckily, Gorillas are very self-aware and can handle any type of person—even men in handlebar mustaches.

Traveling around Europe is something every man, woman, and Gorilla should experience.

Entrusting a Gorilla with Your ATM Pin

*i*f you had a secret that you didn't want anyone else to know, but you just couldn't keep it inside, where would you turn? Your sibling? Your significant other? Your nearest and dearest confidante? Pish posh. If you wanted to keep your secret a secret, you'd tell a Gorilla. That's what you'd do.

Studies have shown that Gorillas, just like humans, are able to retain information and knowledge from past events. A quite useful fact when you consider the need to safeguard something as personal and important as an ATM pin.

Gorillas are sweet and endearing, especially when it comes to safeguarding information about your bank account.

One look at their expressive eyes shows that they clearly understand the implications.

Imagine what it would be like for someone trying to pry a secret from a Gorilla. If you're imagining a man in underwear trying to swim inside a small compartment filled with uncooked oatmeal, you're getting close.

Feel free to entrust a Gorilla with ATM pins, anniversary dates, and security system codes. It's like putting information under an extremely fuzzy lock and key.

Putting Together Furniture with a Gorilla

*i*nvolving a Gorilla is where a task like assembling furniture becomes a lot less like pulling teeth. And a lot more like going down a water slide twenty-five times in an hour, then getting ice cream.

Gorillas have been observed using tools in the wild to further their existence. Of course, this skill set translates well to the furniture assembly process. When putting together furniture with a Gorilla, teamwork is key. Let the Gorilla take the lead, and do as he says.

Most Gorillas tend to like to see what they're working with by laying out all the pieces, then taking a nap. After that, they really get going.

Convoluted instructions are no longer a problem either. Not only do Gorillas think well visually, but they are also fluent in dozens of languages. (Yes, even Igbo.) When it comes to household projects like putting together furniture, don't think of Gorillas as "handy." Think of them as almighty.

Going Clothes
Shopping
with a Gorilla

*i*f you know anything, you know that Gorillas are accomplished bargain hunters. Their decades of experience foraging in steep mountain slopes, river valleys, and meadows can prove invaluable when you're looking for special and unseen gems on a shopping trip to your local mall or thrift store.

If you're shopping with a Gorilla and he suddenly gets excited, let the Gorilla instincts lead you—something is assuredly afoot. Perhaps a rare sweater.

Be sure to limit your shopping outings to once a fortnight—one can only handle so much Gorilla-bargain-hunting-related stimulation.

You can pretty much guarantee a smattering of jealousy from friends once they see your haul from a Gorilla-accompanied shopping trip. Enjoy watching their jaws drop.

Shop with a Gorilla and you'll certainly find some great additions to your wardrobe. Your closet will thank you.

Rapping Alongside a Gorilla Hype Man

*i*n hip hop, the role of a hype man is a crucial one. Hype men must be energetic, without being annoying. Noticeable, without being the center of attention. Engaging, without being distracting. Of course, a Gorilla is all of these things.

Gorillas like to beat their chest in times of excitement. Some of these chest beats, particularly when performed by older male Gorillas, can be quite loud. It's a unique popping sound amplified by air sacs in their chests, which act as an extension of the Gorilla's larynx. Of course, loud chest beating in a hip-hop sense means one very important thing: Gorillas can take the art of beat boxing to cosmic new levels.

Go ahead and start rapping to see the Gorilla hype man at work. Gorillas work the stage well, getting all members of the crowd involved, even (and especially) during outdoor festivals, a time when the attitude of many hip-hop concert-goers might tend toward the more subdued.

Gorillas are masters of the call-and-response chant. Their instructions are brief but fierce, eliciting an immediate reaction from all audience members. Additionally, no one would dare defy a Gorilla when instructed to "Put your hands in the air and wave them like you don't care."

When it's time for your next hip-hop show, look to a Gorilla for your hype man responsibilities. You will not be disappointed.

Taking Self-Defense Lessons from a Gorilla

*d*id you know that Gorillas are experts in all forms of self-defense?

Gorillas are raised to protect their families. Although peaceful and calm by nature, Gorillas will risk their lives in order to protect their family units.

The best thing about learning the art of self-defense from a Gorilla is the fact that you'll learn to use it responsibly, as Gorillas only come to blows as a last resort. That said, when it's time to step it up, Gorillas will do so—in a big way.

Whether your weapon of choice is a nunchaku, blunderbuss, or brass knuckles, when facing off with a Gorilla you will be defeated instantly.

Gorillas have mixed feelings about the UFC and the increasingly popular mixed martial arts battles. They feel it diminishes the sport slightly. They are, however, big fans of Kimbo Slice. He's very marketable, they think.

Upset a Gorilla. See what happens.

On a health kick? Having some vegans over? Company pot-luck coming up? Whatever your reason for making a salad, getting a Gorilla involved is undoubtedly the right decision.

Gorillas live for food. From bark to plant stems to bamboo shoots, Gorillas spend the majority of their lives either searching for food, eating food, or thinking about searching for and eating food. They even have the tendency to fold their goods into little green vegetation sandwiches before chowing down.

Gorillas know where to find the absolute choicest leaves, which is certainly the biggest hurdle when it comes to salad construction. They don't go for that pre-packaged grocery store stuff. They feel it's just plain wrong.

One thing to keep in mind when making a salad with a Gorilla is that the Gorilla will likely eat most of the salad. Consider it a cost of doing business.

Join forces with a Gorilla to make a salad and you'll surely be the talk of your local salad-loving community.

Going Spelunking with a Gorilla

When entering the cold and interesting world of expansive caverns, it's always helpful to have someone with you who knows what they're doing. And if that someone is a large almighty being with an extreme thickness of fur, so much the better.

In recent years, Mountain Gorillas have been observed and photographed entering caves. This phenomenon is believed to be largely due to the rich mineral deposits found within them. Though it could just as easily be a secret lair where Gorillas play poker, throw Frisbees, and ride unicycles—no one really knows for sure.

When you're spelunking down a cave with a Gorilla, be sure to let the Gorilla lead. In fact, it may be best to hitch a ride on the back of your Gorilla companion, as Gorillas have a better sense of direction than over 2,700 GPSs and compasses put together.

You probably thought that an experience of a lifetime would have to involve playing the banjo on a hot air balloon ride, but you would be wrong. Going spelunking with a Gorilla is, in fact, an experience of a lifetime. You should really stop procrastinating.

Video games are like many other aspects of life: fun by yourself, more enjoyable in the company of others. And when by "others" you mean a magnificent specimen of animal that consumes so much vegetation that farmers sweat profusely, well, it's a whole different conversation we're having.

As mentioned, Gorillas have quite impressive dexterity, especially when it comes to their hands and fingers. This is generally useful when eating, as they can slice, dice, and bind to their hearts' content. However, this dexterity extends to feet as well. Imagine for a moment, if you will, the thought of a Gorilla playing, say, *Call of Duty 4*, entirely with his lower appendages. We're talking man-being-shot-out-of-cannon-while-eating-fondue impressive.

But the excitement doesn't end there. Gorillas always maintain positive attitudes, and will root you on until your final boss is defeated, your last world conquered, and your virtual championship won. Just wait until you see what kinds of cheers they come up with.

If you're a gamer, the presence of a Gorilla can only serve to improve your experience—from problem-solving ability to companionship to overall hairiness. In short, when you play video games without a Gorilla, you're only hurting yourself.

*i*f you find yourself in a game of table tennis against the world's greatest mammal, prepare for annihilation. And if you find yourself with a Gorilla as your ping-pong partner, allow us to offer our sincere congratulations in advance.

The key to Gorilla success in ping-pong lies in their hands. It is a fact that Gorilla thumbs are actually smaller than Gorilla fingers, which helps the Gorilla to grip as he climbs trees or grabs foliage.

Essentially, Gorillas have the dexterity of a small army of microscopic robots working inside their skin, which can result in some impressive paddle grips—not to mention some devastating, make-an-opponent-quit-ping-pong-and-immediately-join-the-army spins. Gorillas can hit the ball harder, faster, and with more trajectory than anyone. Just try to get a serve past them.

The only time a Gorilla was defeated in ping-pong was by a Korean in the 1988 Summer Olympics. Gorillas have practiced longer and harder since then, as their moral compasses were shattered by the loss.

Don't expect a Gorilla to lose a ping-pong match again in this lifetime.

Getting a Gorilla to Lead Your Marching Band

*g*orillas are musically adept in a fantastically amazing way. They are also great leaders. This winning combination will help you and your fellow band members excel, hit the right notes, and go on to be famous and earn large bags of money.

Great band leading starts with a great physical presence. Gorillas, and Silverbacks in particular, are known to do a great deal of strutting around. They have a certain way of leaning that makes their arms look gigantic and their bellies quite large. In short, it's a posture sure to get either human or Gorilla attention any time it's struck, and it makes for an awesome presence that any band—from the high school level to an experienced drum and bugle corps—can benefit greatly from.

Even if a Gorilla has never heard your band play before, he can recognize your strengths and weaknesses instantly. To Gorillas, a lot of musical ability can be revealed based on the way you hold your instrument. Posture is an indication of skill. And if you don't have it, they'll know. Boy, will they ever.

Gorillas have been winning music awards internationally for a number of years. They were also close personal friends with both Leonard Cohen and Leonard Bernstein, and several Gorillas also served as technical advisers for the major motion picture *Drumline*. If you don't think that gives them cred in the marching-band world, God help you.

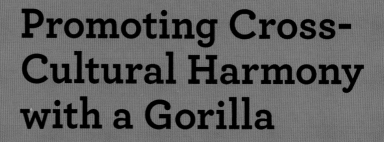

Promoting Cross-Cultural Harmony with a Gorilla

*t*hough impressive in stature (the understatement of the millennium), Gorillas try to minimize the use of force at all costs. This may occasionally, but not always, involve bamboo.

When disagreements occur, Gorillas often turn to a useful standby—submissive gestures. This helps the Gorilla diffuse things immediately, and communicates to their potential adversary that they are not a threat. Smart. Gorillas realize how easy it is to misinterpret hand gestures. For that reason, each hand signal they use is accompanied by a deep grunt of affirmation, making the meaning of that particular gesture crystal clear.

Gorillas also have a knack for communicating without words or gestures. How do they do this, you ask? Through their eyes, which seem to be saying, "I understand you. Also, you look quite nice in that top." This helps in matters of cross-cultural communication because their gentle stares can break through any language barrier.

Having their fuzzy fingers on the pulse of world culture trends puts Gorillas in an optimal position to diffuse potential powder kegs of miscommunication—large, small, and anywhere in between.

When it comes to promoting cross-cultural harmony, understanding, and communications, Gorillas do have an underlying philosophy: When all else fails, resort to bamboo.

Barbecuing with a Gorilla

*f*act: Gorillas are experts at food preparation. Due to all the vegetation they consume, they generally try to prepare it in a variety of unique manners by folding leaves, trimming bark by hand and mouth, making sandwiches, and foraging with their hands.

With this expansive knowledge of food preparation, it should be no surprise that Gorillas make fantastic Grill Masters. Despite their vegetarian leanings, Gorillas are highly skilled at preparing your steaks, chops, burgers, dogs, mini sliders, and cutlets in a highly efficient and always tasty manner.

Gorillas don't need to use tongs when grilling—they can just turn the meat by hand. Gorillas can't get burned, as their hands are protected with a robust layer of awesome. Low-land Gorillas make the best Gorilla Grill Masters, as their coats are suited for warm forest habitats. As a result, they have no problem being near the hot grill, even for extended periods of time. Gorillas have the endurance and strength of many, many firefighters, with or without their hoses.

When you enlist a Gorilla to help man the grill so you can learn all his amazing techniques at your next barbecue, you can be certain that the responsibility will be handled with the utmost care, grace, and skill. In other words: yum.

Having a Gorilla Plan Your Wedding

When it's time to tie the knot, look to a Gorilla to provide you with the kindness, support, and instruction you need to plan the happiest day of your life.

Gorillas generally possess a calm demeanor. They don't get riled up easily, and their temperament is very relaxed. This steady, and not to mention extremely dexterous, hand serves Gorillas well in all aspects of wedding planning, from cake tasting to choosing a photographer to tying bows on chair covers.

Just for kicks, it's sometimes fun to attempt to become a bridezilla around a Gorilla. The steely eye you'll receive in return is akin to a harpoon to the left clavicle.

Hiring a Gorilla to be your wedding planner will ensure the special-est of special days—especially if you invite the Gorilla to be part of your wedding photos. They really appreciate that. You should also know that Gorilla ministers are becoming increasingly more common at weddings. David and Victoria Beckham's, for example.

Besides weddings, Gorillas are also strong supporters of civil unions.

VANILLA WHITE YELLOW

A. Gorilla

60,473,826,052,714,081 Followers

▼ see all

Becoming a Gorilla's Social Network Connection

gorillas are social animals by nature. And this socialization easily extends to the online space.

Gorillas thrive on the ability to be social creatures. Interacting with each other, whether nonverbally or through a series of grunts, helps them decide where to forage, where to sleep, and what to do. In addition, Gorillas are known to frequently change social groups, whether it's to jockey for a better mating position, get on the fast track to becoming the leader of their own group, or just enjoy a change of scenery—and different-but-similar-tasting leaves. These groups can vary from numbers as small as just a few to as large as fifty or more, meaning Gorillas are not just socially apt, but socially versatile as well.

Gorillas are known to frequent all major online social networking channels, from Facebook to LinkedIn to WAYN.

Any time you come across Gorillas on one of these websites, it would behoove you to friend them. Gorillas are tuned into the latest news, bulletins, social gatherings, and job offers in a way that you could only hope to be. The more Gorilla friends, the better.

If you are nervous about asking a Gorilla you don't know very well to be a social networking connection, don't be. Gorillas are very understanding and inclusive, and they know that they can benefit you in some way through a connection, real or imagined. Think of them as really fuzzy community organizers.

Befriending Gorillas through your social network will keep you connected to everything you could ever want or need. Particularly in the vegetation department.

Having a Gorilla Help You with Your Homework

*h*istory question? Calculus query? Essay to write? Look no further. Gorillas are well educated in pretty much every subject, and will graciously help you with your homework so you can get it turned in on time—and earn a gold star for your efforts.

Gorillas are considered highly intelligent animals. You may have heard about a few that have been taught sign language.

If it were the 1950s, this rare combination of beauty and brains would result in expressions from onlookers like "that Gorilla is so dreamy!" Incidentally, Gorillas are so entrancing that sometimes this expression is still uttered, even today.

While Gorillas are versed in all subjects, they have a particular affinity for math. They enjoy tackling problems with an order and exact, regimented conclusion. Which is funny, because they are also prone to abstract thinking on a regular basis too. Some have it all. Like Gorillas.

In addition to being walking, hairy encyclopedias for all your homework needs, Gorillas are also masters of take home tests. Provided you don't let them eat the paper.

Organizing an Olympic-Caliber Bobsled Team with a Gorilla

Since birth, the strength and agility training Gorillas have received as a result of living in rainforests and mountains is surely of Olympic caliber. In these environments, Gorillas are able to develop the strength to stay steady and balanced, enabling them to plow ahead at high speeds—even in very dense vegetation. Therefore, putting a Gorilla on a closed course in a bobsled is truly a no-brainer.

Gorillas have a knack for memorizing the twists and turns, however bendy, of all bobsled courses. Plus, they have a foolproof communication method: They grunt when it's time to turn. You, assuming you're wise, will listen.

The thick fur of a Mountain Gorilla provides insulation against the extreme cold, meaning no uniform for your Gorilla bobsledder. And therefore, better aerodynamics.

Gorillas like to mat down their fur with a fine gel or paste prior to sled runs—it makes them faster. They find that the best way to do this is with Miracle Whip.

Imagine the endorsement possibilities of a Gorilla-helmed bobsled team. Your sled would most likely be painted to look like a giant banana, so iconic it could be viewed from miles away.

There are numerous Gorilla gold medalists living among us today. After seeing the visionary possibilities of one in a bobsled, it's not hard to see why. Wheaties should be calling any minute.

Having a Gorilla Lead Your Tour Group

With such a breadth of personalities crammed into a single location, tour groups can be decidedly hit or miss. The best way to ensure a memorable tour group experience is to make sure a Gorilla is leading it.

Gorillas are some of the most experienced group leaders in the business. Gorillas are known for their ability to keep a group intact and satisfied. When searching for food in the wild, Gorillas will wait for other group members, making sure everyone sticks together. Gorilla groups will also slow down when a member is sick or injured, maintaining an amazing sense of both unity and humanity.

Gorillas have the right blend of humor and knowledge to keep your touring experience both lighthearted and educational. Gone are the typical corny tour jokes like "What's brown and sticky?" (A stick.) Gorillas tend to have a more highbrow sense of humor reminiscent of Stephen Colbert, John Hodgman, and Sting.

Gorilla-led tour groups also minimize the razzle-dazzle in favor of a more authentic experience. Throughout your tour, you will notice fewer money-suck attempts, like paying for posed pictures or having assorted trinkets, knick-knacks, and novelty cups for sale. Gorillas would rather focus on the experience itself.

Be sure to tip your Gorilla guide at the end of what will undoubtedly be the best tour you will have ever experienced. All measures of plants, bark, and tree branches are preferable.

Having a Gorilla Umpire
Your Next Baseball Game

When it's time to bring an impartial, large, and talented overseer to the baseball diamond, look no further than our big, hairy friends.

Gorillas have been watching and playing baseball since Abner Doubleday invented it in the late 1880s. Maybe even prior to that.

As an authority figure, Gorillas obviously bring a lot to the table. In the wild, Silverbacks tend to remain impartial—it's the only way to keep peace with the many females that compete for their affections.

No one will ever attempt to scream, yell, or kick dirt on the shoes of a Gorilla, making the baseball game much more pleasant. It's also always fun to see if any of the players will try to bump a Gorilla ump, only to be subsequently found lying in a pool of their own filth.

Gorillas also have entertaining calls for strikes and outs, as they tend to gesticulate and hoot assuredly with many parts of their body. Baseball's entertainment factor just went through the roof.

A Gorilla umpire: judge, jury, and prosecutor. Fuzzy, fuzzy prosecutor.

Hiring a Gorilla to Be Your Fashion Consultant

gorillas have the patience, the expertise, and the where-withal to be fashion gurus to anyone in the world, regardless of their size, color preference, or favorite cattle breed.

Many consultants in the fashion world are notoriously diffi-cult and/or arrogant. Not so in this case. Gorillas are known for their ability to roll with the punches. If they get annoyed, they tend not to make a scene. More often than not, they choose a gentle rebuff, rather than a full-on display of Gorilla displeasure. This ability to not sweat the small stuff is perfect for the arena of dealing with meltdowns by would-be fashion aficionados, acid-washed-based tantrums, and the hysterics of those with a stubborn affinity for pleats.

In addition, Gorillas know just about everything about the current fashions of any country—from Japan's kimonos to Ghana's dashikis. Just be careful when it's time for them to demonstrate a proper runway walk. Their massiveness could destroy the entire Milan runway.

Once a Gorilla walks through your door in a dapper suit and tie to help you with your fashion makeover, you'll never want him to leave. Consider enrolling your kids in the "Apes and Ascots" extended fashion education program. If you apply now, you're guaranteed placement by 2045.

Working with a Gorilla to Maximize Your Downtime

gorillas are the best downtime-enjoyers ever created. Did you ever wonder who first mastered that whole couch-with-a-mini-fridge-and-bowl-of-pretzels-in-its-false-wall invention? No, it wasn't Mike Ditka. It was our larger, more expressive, celery-consuming compatriots—it was, in fact, Gorillas.

Though amazingly productive, Gorillas can lie around for days, even weeks, at a time—and they frequently do. While often done in the midst of their family groups, Gorillas also like to relax for long periods on their own, as it's the best way to sprawl out and avoid the pressures of the day. Many young Gorillas will spend hours on their own, playing, discovering, and relaxing by twirling, rolling in vegetation, and even spinning aimlessly. Good times.

Here's a tip: Swing from vines and try eating some bark. Whether or not you develop a taste for wood or vegetation is not important—it's more the idea of trying new and different things that is pertinent here, in order to allow for maximum relaxation and carefree-ness.

Lessons gleaned from these solo play and relaxation periods can be put to good use when it comes to things like running companies, organizing chili cook-offs, and writing memoirs. When you relax like a Gorilla, the mind begins to find, and sometimes even grow, new chambers of knowledge, wisdom, and understanding. It's scientific fact.

The World Is Better with Gorillas

Due to factors like poaching and loss of natural habitat, the world Gorilla population is dangerously low—currently, Gorillas are one of the world's most endangered species. Please help these magnificent Great Apes by giving generously to one of the organizations listed here. Together, we can help give Gorillas what they truly deserve—a chance at living their lives happily and leisurely.

Friends of Gorillas

Please visit any of the following websites to find out how you can help contribute to the survival of great apes.

Mountain Gorilla Veterinary Project
Gorilladoctors.org

The Dian Fossey Gorilla Fund International
Gorillafund.org

Virunga National Park
Gorillacd.org

Wildlife Direct
Wildlifedirect.org

The Gorilla Foundation
Koko.org

African Wildlife Foundation
Awf.org

GRASP—Great Apes Survival Partnership
Unep.org/grasp

The Year of the Gorilla
Yog2009.org

IGCP—International Gorilla Conservation Program
gcp.org

Fauna and Flora International
Fauna-flora.org

Gearing Up for Gorillas
G4g.co.uk

Gorilla Haven
Gorilla-haven.org

About the Author

Andrew Gall currently works as an advertising copywriter for independent Seattle ad agency/digital hub HL2, where he writes and concepts for a wide range of clients. Prior to that, he worked in Chicago for ad agency Cramer Krasselt. Andrew's advertising work has been recognized by a number of advertising publications, including *Communication Arts*, *Creativity*, *Adweek*, *Graphis*, and *Luerzer's Archive*. He enjoys running, reading, and being consumed by all forms of media. He currently lives in Seattle with his wife Megan, and can be reached at *andrew.gall@gmail.com*. This is his first book.

One day, he hopes to trek the Gorillas in Rwanda, Uganda, and the Democratic Republic of Congo.

About the Gorillastrator

Vince Soliven has been designing, art directing, and illustrating projects of all sorts for a number of years. Originally from Hawaii, Vince moved stateside to begin his advertising career as an art director at famed agency Cramer Krasselt in Chicago, Illinois. After a number of years there, Vince has since relocated to M&CSaatchi Los Angeles. His work has been recognized by several distinguished advertising journals, including *Communication Arts*, *Creativity*, *Adweek*, *Graphis*, and *Luerzer's Archive*. He enjoys snakes (two-headed ones are a plus), music, art, and also has a special interest in Rube Goldberg machines. He currently resides in Los Angeles with his wife Shaleah, daughter Sydney, and two chihuahuas.

Vince has collaborated on a number of projects with Andrew, Gorilla-related and otherwise.

Photo by Bryan "Oh, Bryan™" Dixon